> " Modern Vaudeville Press is changing the game – they are setting a new standard for circademics around the world [in their commitment] to writing entertaining books that don't sacrifice academic scrutiny.
> -the International Jugglers' Association "

For wholesale inquiries, contact:
wholesale@modernvaudevillepress.com

For all other inquiries, contact:
info@modernvaudevillepress.com

www.modernvaudevillepress.com

Modern Vaudeville Press Catalogue
ISBN – 978-1-958604-21-2

Modern Vaudeville Press Catalogue

Updated Summer 2025

Books

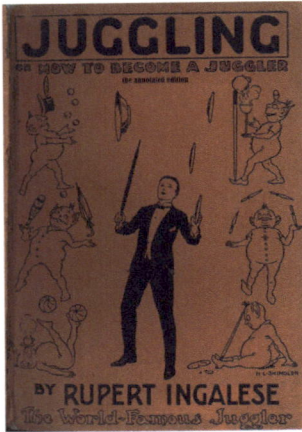

Juggling: Or How to Become a Juggler (annotated edition)

Rupert Ingalese, annotated by Thom Wall
ISBN – 978-1733971201
99 pages
MSRP: $15 USD

The fully annotated edition of Rupert Ingalese's 1921 "how to juggle" manual. This book covers basic juggling technique, tricks with hats and canes, practice methodology, and more. Ingalese's manuscript provides an interesting look at the state of juggling pedagogy in Britain's music hall era. Annotations by juggler and circus researcher Thom Wall bring insight and context to Ingalese's descriptions and instructions.

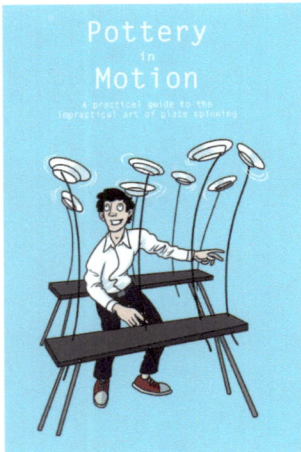

Pottery in Motion

Sam Veale
ISBN – 978-1733971232
71 pages
MSRP: $15 USD

British juggler Sam Veale's *Pottery in Motion* is the first of its kind - a straightforward book that provides aspiring plate spinners both the specifics of the props (such as plates, sticks, and rack) and comprehensive instruction on the skill of plate spinning itself. This small but detail-packed guide appeals to individuals looking to learn plate spinning and provides the knowledge to take it to a performance-ready level, just add practice.

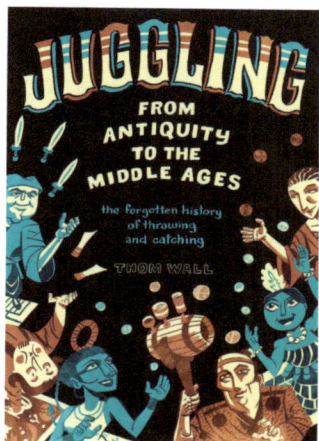

Juggling: From Antiquity to the Middle Ages

Thom Wall
ISBN – 978-0578410845
e-book ISBN – 978-0578410852
129 pages
MSRP: $25 USD

As with dance, so with juggling—the moment that the performer finishes the routine, their act ceases to exist beyond the memory of the audience. There is no permanent record of what transpired, so studying the ancient roots of juggling is fraught with difficulty. Using the records that do exist, juggling appears to have emerged around the world in cultures independent of one another in the ancient past. Paintings in Egypt from 2000 BCE show jugglers engaged in performance. Stories from the island nation of Tonga place juggling's creation with their goddess of the underworld—a figure who has guarded a cave since time immemorial. Juggling games and rituals are pervasive in isolated Inuit cultures in northern Canada and Greenland. Though the earliest representation of juggling is 4,000 years old, the practice is surely much older—in the same way that humans were doubtlessly singing and dancing long before the first bone flute was created.

This book is an attempt to catalogue this tangible history of juggling in human culture. It is the story of juggling, represented in art and writing from around the world, across time. Although much has been written about modern jugglers–specific performers, their props, and their routines–little has been said about those who first developed the craft. As juggling enters a golden age in the internet era, *Juggling: From Antiquity to the Middle Ages* offers a look into the past—to the origins of our art form.

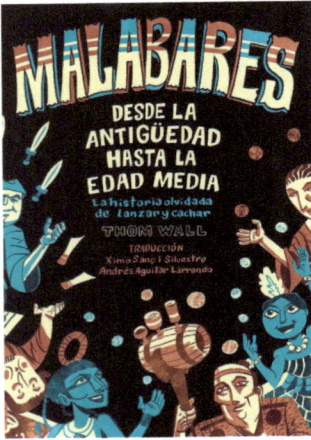

Spanish Edition:

Malabares - desde la Antigüedad hasta la Edad Media: la historia olvidada de lanzar y cachar

Thom Wall, et. al.
ISBN – 978-1733971263
e-book ISBN – 978-1958604007
179 pages
MSRP: $25 USD

Malabares - desde Antigüedad hasta la Edad Media, es un divertido viaje por países, por épocas. Desde el Antiguo Egipto y sus ya famosas malabaristas profesionales de la tumba nº 15 de Beni Hasan, a los juegos para niñas de la isla de Tonga y otras zonas del Pacífico Sur; pasando por los edictos del rey Alfonso X de Castilla sobre la regulación de los juglares o los antipodistas aztecas actuando ante el Papa Clemente VII en el siglo XVI. También reserva un espacio al final del libro para, aprovechando su faceta de lingüista, realizar unas reflexiones acerca de la propia definición de la palabra "juggling"[malabarismo] a lo largo del tiempo y sus orígenes. Es, por tanto, un libro ideal no solo para malabaristas o cirqueros, sino para cualquiera con curiosidad sobre la historia, en especial de aquellos hechos que en ocasiones pasan más desapercibidos en los textos cotidianos.

A través de este libro aprendemos sobre leyendas y juegos antiguos, fantaseamos con grandes artistas y actuaciones que nunca podremos ver y que nos hacen dudar sobre esa tan manida sentencia que a veces afirma "esto nunca se ha hecho antes".
- *Malabares en su Tinta*

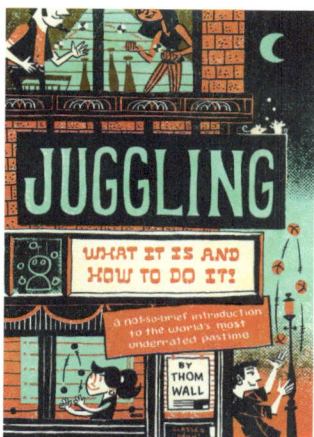

Juggling: What It Is and How to Do It

Thom Wall, et. al.
ISBN – 978-1-7339712-5-6
e-book ISBN – 978-1-7339712-8-7
224 pages
MSRP: $25 USD

Juggling: What It Is and How to Do It teaches learners of all ages how to juggle – one of the world's oldest artforms. With a kind demeanor, humor, and enthusiasm, this authoritative manual explains the process of juggling through four different modalities, bolstered by the latest physical education research.

Juggling is an accessible primer that a middle-schooler can hit the ground running with, or that families can enjoy together. The result of six years of work by 2021 International Jugglers' Association *Excellence in Education* award winner and former Cirque du Soleil juggler Thom Wall and featuring guest chapters by some of today's juggling masters, *Juggling* provides great content for even the most serious adult learner.

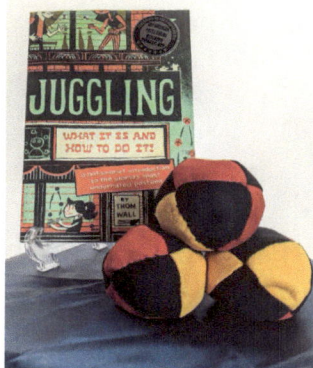

Book plus Juggling Kit!
Includes juggling balls by Alchemy Juggling

MSRP: $60 USD

This exclusive kit makes the perfect gift for any aspiring juggler. Includes one copy of *Juggling: What It Is and How to Do It* and three professional-grade beanbags.

Beanbag specs: 90g ea., approx. 2.75" diameter. Machine washable / dryable. Made in USA.

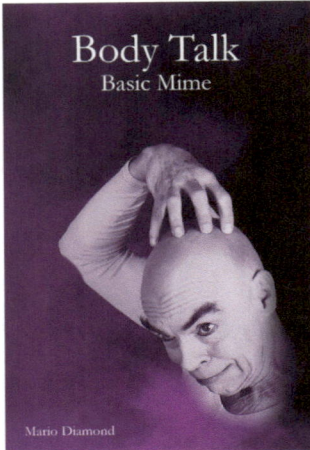

Body Talk: Basic Mime

Mario Diamond
ISBN – 978-1733971218
73 pages
MSRP: $15 USD

Body Talk: Basic Mime covers the fundamental skills of mime in an easily accessible workbook format. Diamond brings over 40 years of teaching and performance experience to *Body Talk*, which includes rich photography illustrating various mime techniques.

"[*Body Talk: Basic Mime*] should be required reading for any theater participant looking to incorporate elements of mime into their routines." - *Midwest Book Review*

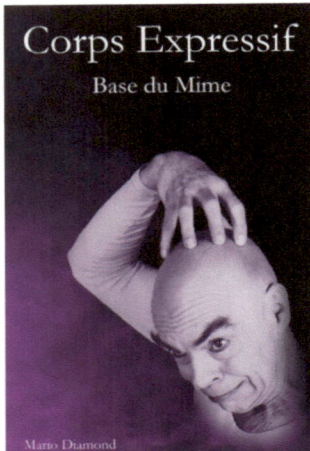

French Edition:
Corps Expressif: Base du Mime

Mario Diamond
ISBN – 978-1958604984
68 pages
MSRP: $15 USD

Mario a écrit un tour de force sur l'art du mime. Ce livre est éloquent et concis... riche en outils pour les élèves comme pour les professeurs, facile à comprendre et rempli d'exercices pratiques. Ce livre est brodé de segments historiques et anecdotiques qui en font un manuscrit amusant, plein d'observations charmantes et bouffonnes qui font de Mario un artiste phénoménal, prodigue de la caractéristique définitive du mime, la personnalité.

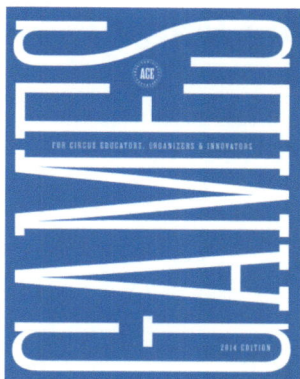

Circus Games (v1.1)

Compiled by Lucy Little & the American Youth Circus Organization (AYCO)
ISBN – 9781733971225
e-book ISBN – 978-1-958604-01-4
124 pages
MSRP: $15 USD

With over 100 games organized for optimal use in cooperative movement based settings, this is a must have for every circus school, teaching artist, and arts education program! Games are organized by age, number of participants, energy level, and social/emotional learning outcome, and also includes special notes for working with a variety of populations that may require adaptation or modifications to each game. Find more info about the project here:
https://www.americancircuseducators.org/gamesproject/

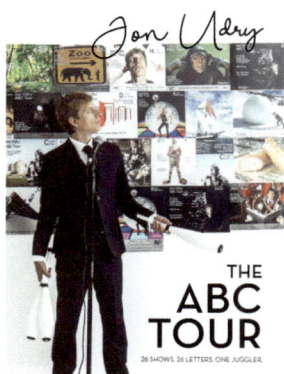

The ABC Tour

Jon Udry
ISBN – 978-0578410852
MSRP: $25 USD

Ever felt like a challenge? For juggler and comedian, Jon Udry, the ABC Tour — 26 letters, 26 shows — seems the perfect way to shake things up. What started as a silly idea he believed would take two to three months to complete, ended up being a mammoth three year project that included some of the toughest, most brutal and most enjoyable performances of his life. From attempting to juggle while wearing roller skates and the unexpected discoveries of performing at a Naturist's Resort, to the challenges that came with working in rainforest conditions covered in ants or in snowy conditions at -10°C, Jon tells the full story from A to Z.

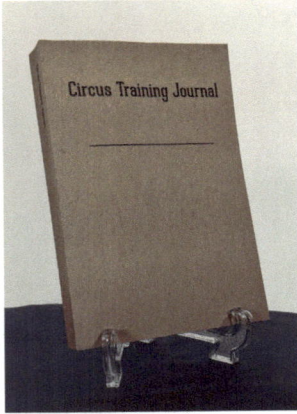

Circus Training Journal

Thom Wall & Rebecca Starr,
Consultant editor: Sarah Baker
ISBN – 978-1-7339712-9-4
9×6" paperback
380 pages
MSRP: $20 USD

What's measured is managed! The *Circus Training Journal* is the result of a year of collaboration between Thom Wall and Rebecca Starr, aerial coach. This undated journal, spanning three months of daily training, tracks workouts, nutrition, goal-setting, and more. Heavyweight paper optimized for ballpoint and pencil.

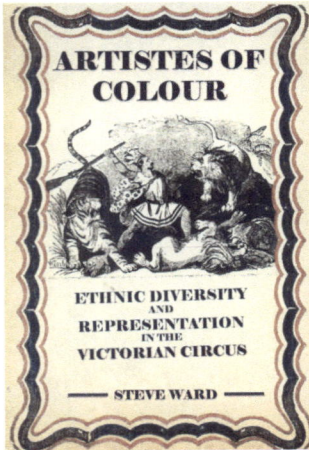

Artistes of Colour

Steve Ward, PhD
ISBN – 978-1-7339712-7-0
e-book ISBN – 978-1-958604-99-1
317 pages
MSRP: $25 USD

In a society that places an increasing value in ethnic diversity and cultural identity, the contribution that performers from a variety of ethnic backgrounds made to the development of the circus in the nineteenth century is often dismissed and largely forgotten. Using contemporary records and images, *Artistes of Colour* explores the wealth and depth of talented black and other performers of colour, and their contributions to the success of the nineteenth century circus. Ward draws iconic figures from the margins of history and gives them the recognition they deserve. Long-listed for the American Society for Theatre Research 2022 Book Award.

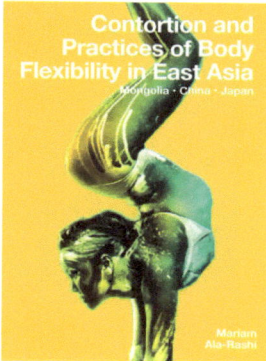

Contortion and Practices of Body Flexibility in East Asia - Mongolia, China, Japan

Mariam Ala-Rashi
ISBN – 978-1-958604-04-5
e-book ISBN – 978-1-958604-06-9
464 pages
MSRP: $25 USD

A collection of three monographs: *China's Bending Bodies: Contortionists and Politics in China*; *Mongolian Contortion: An Ethnographic Inquiry*; and *The Kakubei Jishi: The Rise, Fall, and Restoration of a Japanese Folk Performing Art.*

This compendium examines contortion and practices of body flexibility in East Asia. It explores the performance art forms Chinese contortion, Mongolian contortion and the Kakubei Jishi lion dance of the Niigata prefecture in Japan which utilizes body flexibility. It discusses the investigation of the history and genesis of these art forms and how they developed in various political and social dynamics. This work further offers vast knowledge about crucial elements such as the artist's training processes, their training environment, the development of aesthetics, symbolism in costuming and body movements, religious themes, mythology and natural phenomena, and costume designs. This compendium includes data from a wide range of literature, material evidence, oral history, current media reports, and considers recent work in anthropology, archaeology, and political history. It offers the interested reader, the scholar, the contortionist and contortion practitioner a substantial treatise about contortionism and practices of body flexibility.

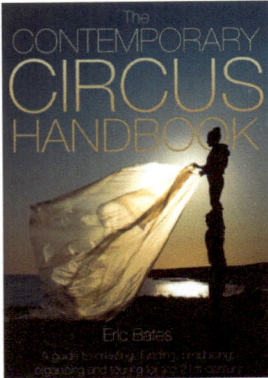

The Contemporary Circus Handbook: A guide to creating, funding, producing, organizing and touring shows for the 21st century

Eric Bates
ISBN – 978-1-958604-03-8
e-book ISBN – 978-1-958604-18-2
374 pages
MSRP: $25 USD

The Contemporary Circus Handbook contains interviews with more than 25 professionals, from Gypsy Snider of the celebrated contemporary circus company The Seven Fingers to Lydia Bouchard of La Resistance about their work in the performing arts world. Combining Eric Bates' (Cie Barcode, Cirque du Soleil, et. al.) hard won wisdom as well as tips and insights from his contemporaries, what emerges is an invaluable blueprint of how to progress from the seed of an idea for a show to the full touring timeline. The scope of the book is wide but deeply hands-on, diving into practical details on how to find an agent, start your own company, secure funding and build your niche brand. *The Contemporary Circus Handbook* truly is a unique offering to the circus world, full of insider tips and years of accumulated knowledge from industry insiders.

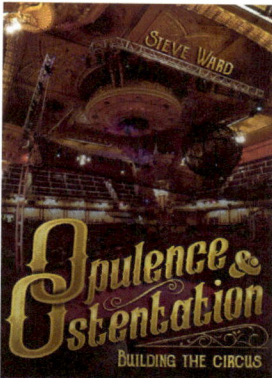

Opulence & Ostentation

Steve Ward, PhD
ISBN – 978-1-958604-02-1
e-book ISBN – 978-1-958604-05-2
247 pages
MSRP: $25 USD

Since the foundation of 'modern' circus in the 18th century, the circus has been presented in defined spaces. Initially, performances were given in the open air and, over a period of time, these spaces first became enclosed and then later roofed. In the 19th century, many permanent stone-built buildings were erected solely for presenting circus. This phenomenon spread from the UK across Europe and beyond, creating a style of circus architecture that has never been repeated. This book examines what caused these buildings to be constructed and their design and architectur, including some still being used for circus performances today. The book also looks at the developments of contemporary circus architecture and raise questions as to the future of the circus building.

Cleverer Than God

Erik Åberg
ISBN – 978-1958604113
116 pages
MSRP: $25 USD

Cleverer Than God is a book that tells the story of Paul Cinquevalli, a juggler who rose from the Circus circuit of the 1880s, to attain celebrity status in the British Music Hall and American vaudeville stages until the outbreak of WWI. Through quotes by Cinquevalli himself, woven together with excerpts from journalists and writers of his era, the book tells his story as poignant fragments, capturing the essence of Cinquevalli's triumphs, defining moments, and heart-rending tragedies.

BADGE BOOK

*Youth Juggling
Academy*

The Juggler's Badge Book

Author: Benjamin Domask-Ruh
Editors: Thayer Slichter, Afton Benson
Illustrators: Thayer Slichter and Louis Skaradek
ISBN – 978-1-958604-19-9
MSRP: $25 USD

Introducing *The Juggler's Badge Book*, the ultimate companion for aspiring jugglers! Track your progress, unlock achievements, and earn badges as you learn the art of juggling. With its engaging format and rewarding sticker system, *The Juggler's Badge Book* makes learning to juggle an exciting and fulfilling adventure. Whether you're a beginner or a seasoned juggler, let *The Juggler's Badge Book* be your guide to skillful juggling and a collection of well-earned accomplishments. Start achieving your juggling journey today with this activity book from the Youth Juggling Academy, a program of the International Jugglers' Association!

Published in collaboration between the
International Jugglers' Association and Modern Vaudeville Press.

By Royal Command: Barnum in Europe

Steve Ward, PhD
ISBN – 978-1-958604-26-7
e-book ISBN – 978-1-958604-27-4
240 pages
MSRP: $25 USD

On a cold February day in 1844, a small group of travellers disembarked their ship in Liverpool, England. Amongst them was the American showman P. T. Barnum and his protégé Charles S. Stratton, known as General Tom Thumb. This marked the beginning of a three-year long tour of the United Kingdom and continental Europe that would bring both Barnum and Stratton international fame and fortune.

By Royal Command charts the progress of this tour, with all its triumphs and disasters, and examines the impact Barnum and Tom Thumb had on social attitudes towards the 'exotic'.

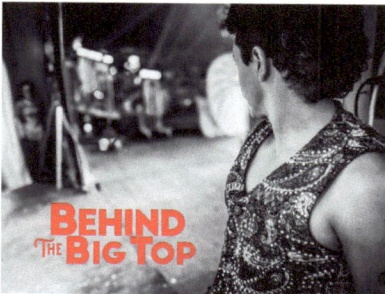

Behind the Big Top: A Photo Exploration of Circus Flora 2024

Ryan Stanley
ISBN – 978-1-958604-29-8
MSRP: $25 USD

Ryan Stanley set out to photograph Circus Flora from start to finish, capturing its unique essence. Meet fantastic performers, crew members, and volunteers who created a sense of community that felt like family. The images in this book showcase the magical moments of the circus along with the behind-the-scenes work that brings it to life.

After dedicating countless hours to this project, Stanley gained a new appreciation for Circus Flora and the Circus Arts. Join him for a behind-the-scenes look at Circus Flora 2024 - Start to Finish.

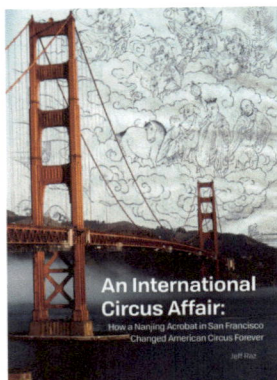

An International Circus Affair:
How a Nanjing Acrobat in San Francisco Changed American Circus Forever

Jeff Raz
ISBN – 978-1-958604-24-3
e-book ISBN – 978-1-958604-25-0
311 pages
MSRP: $25 USD

In 1989, the Artistic Director of a San Francisco circus, Judy Finelli, met briefly with Lu Yi, the Director of the Nanjing Acrobatic Troupe, in upstate New York. It was, as Judy now calls it, "a moment that changed circus forever." Lu Yi would move to San Francisco to teach the 2000-year-old art of Chinese acrobatics.

This book looks at the 20 years after Lu Yi's arrival and how his acrobatic training and his students' prowess changed San Francisco and Nanjing, as well as circuses around the world.

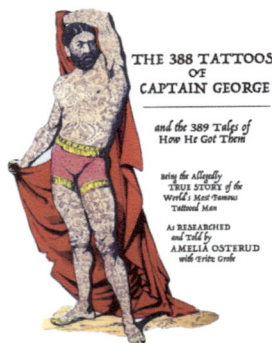

The 388 Tattoos of Captain George and the 389 Tales of How He Got Them:
Being the allegedly true story of the world's most famous tattooed man, as researched and told by Amelia Osterud with Fritz Grobe

Amelia Osterud with Fritz Grobe
ISBN – coming soon
e-book ISBN – coming soon
MSRP: $25 USD

He appeared out of the blue in Vienna, covered from head to toe in hundreds of Burmese tattoos. Then, as the Golden Age of American circus began, P. T. Barnum made him the most famous tattooed performer of all time. He said he had been a pirate and a patriot, a rebel and a slave. He claimed he had been tortured by an evil Tatar despot, tattooed by a vengeful sailor in Kashgar, and inked by a princess in Turkistan. Captain George Costentenus told so many outrageous and conflicting tales – what is the truth?

Over
★★★ **8,000** ★★★
kits donated
so far!

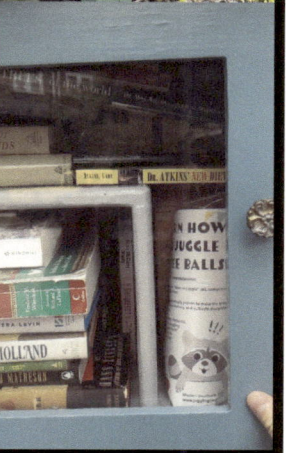

Make a difference by sponsoring...

★ The World's ★
Newest Juggler!

★

Each kit contains a set of three juggling balls and a booklet of beginner juggling instructions. Sponsor a new kit today!

"To the kind person who left the beginner's kit in the Little Library on Wonderland Drive - Thank you. You made my day! I had earlier in the day joked to myself about all the new hobbies I started to fill my time since COVID. I joked to myself that I should take up juggling. During my run later, I poked my head in the Little Library and discovered the kit. Made me laugh. Thank you. Thank you." -M.S.

"Thanks to all of you, something beautiful has come into the world. Times are hard, and especially challenging for children who are facing huge disruptions to their lives at home and at school. Things like these juggling kits can feel like gifts from a kind world to some of these people." -anonymous

Find out more at www.modernvaudevillepress.com/sponsor

Find Our Books Here!

MVP is proud to be a part of the follow associations:

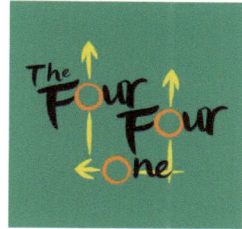

MVP Mission

Modern Vaudeville Press is a mission-driven, artist-owned independent publishing company. We strive to build a platform for unique nonfiction titles in juggling, circus, vaudeville, and related fields. MVP aims to drive the conversation about circus forward by increasing accessibility to high-quality titles about the history and instruction of circus arts.

Our award-winning books are carried in shops on four continents, as well as by many large online retailers.

Notes about Packaging

We at MVP take the environment and its stewardship seriously. Whenever possible, orders will be shipped in recycled or re-used envelopes, packages, and bubble mailers. Some orders might be delivered in multiple shipments, depending on supply chains.

www.ingramcontent.com/pod-product-compliance
Lightning Source LLC
Chambersburg PA
CBHW042131040426
42335CB00035B/199